# CAT BREEDS

# CAT BREEDS

## The new compact study guide and identifier

Paddy Cutts

CHARTWELL
BOOKS, INC.

A QUINTET BOOK

Published by Chartwell Books
A Division of Book Sales, Inc.
PO Box 7100
Edison, New Jersey 08818-7100

This edition produced for sale
in the U.S.A., its territories
and dependencies only.

ISBN 0-7858-0325-4

This book was designed and produced by
Quintet Publishing Limited
6 Blundell Street
London N7 9BH

Creative Director: Richard Dewing
Designer: Ian Hunt
Project Editor: Claire Tennant-Scull
Editor: Lesley Ellis
All photographs © Animals Unlimited/Paddy Cutts
except 24, 25, 28 (below), 44, 48 (above)
54 (above and below) and 58 above © Larry Johnson.

Typeset in Great Britain by
Central Southern Typesetters, Eastbourne
Manufactured by Bright Arts (Pte) Ltd, Singapore
Printed by Star Standard Industries (Pte) Ltd, Singapore

Acknowledgement:
Paddy Cutts would like to thank the Colour Centre
London for processing the photographs with their
usual care and efficiency.

# CONTENTS

# INTRODUCTION

From their humble beginnings as semi-domesticated mousers, cats have become probably our most popular domestic pets, and not without good reason. Unlike dogs, they do not vary greatly in size from one breed to another, or do they require regular, lengthy walks. They are fastidiously clean little animals, spending a good part of their day washing and preening their coats, and even their toilet habits can be confined to a litter tray, making them ideal companions for anyone living in a flat or apartment.

However, not all cat breeds are suited to every environment or household and some have most specific requirements, so you should give careful consideration to the breed you select.

Longhaired breeds, though generally easy-going and undemanding, need a considerable amount of time spent on grooming. If this is not done regularly for at least 10–15 minutes each day, their coats soon become matted, which is both un-

comfortable for the cat and expensive for the owner when the vet's bill for dematting comes in.

While shorthaired breeds require only the minimum of extra grooming, they can be demanding in other, possibly more annoying ways. This is particularly true of Burmese, Orientals and Siamese – once heard, the Siamese voice is never forgotten.

Russians and Korats tend to be quiet breeds, whilst the Rex breeds are often mischievous. The Turkish, with its love of swimming, prefers a home with a swimming pool, but it can make do with a dip in the bath-tub!

Remember that cats can live for 18 years or more, which can seem like an eternity if you select the wrong breed. Do not be swayed by looks alone, but consider the cat's inner needs too – make the right choice, and you and your cat should live in harmony for many years.

## COATS

There are many types of coat texture, and an even greater number of colours and patterns. In general, the solid colours are referred to as "self colours" and the patterned coats as "non-self". The Persian coat is long and thick, but soft and fine to the touch; the Maine Coon has a semi-long coat with a waterproof finish; "tipped" coats have a pale undercoat with just the tops of each hair tipped with colour; the Abyssinian is an excellent example of an agouti ticked coat; the Siamese has the "Himalayan" coat pattern, with colour restricted to the points; and the Rex is a curly-coated variety, with little undercoat.

**Blue Persian**

**Maine Coon**

**British Tipped**

**Rex-Cornish**

**Siamese**

**Abyssinian**

## EYES

Cats' eyes vary in shape from the full, round eyes of the Persian, to the inscrutable oriental shape of the Siamese. The Persian has large, round, full eyes which are usually deep copper coloured; the semi-longhaired Birman has large eyes, but less round and bold than the Persian; the Burmilla has a slightly oriental eye set which is neither almond nor round; and the Siamese has deep sapphire-blue eyes of oriental shape.

**Persian**

**British**

**Birman**

**Siamese**

**Birmilla**

## EARS

These range from small and neat, to large and flared. The Persian has small, neat, well-furnished ears that are wide-set; the Norwegian Forest Cat has wide-based, high-set ears with lynx-like tufts; Burmese have medium-sized ears, wide-set with slightly rounded tips; and the Siamese has large, pricked ears that are wide-set at the base.

**Persian**

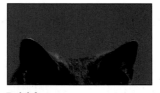

**British**

**Norweigian Forest Cat**

**Siamese**

**Brown Burmese**

## HEADS

Head shapes range from the round, short-faced Persian, to the long, angular Siamese. The Persian has a round, broad-skulled head with a short face, and in profile shows a distinct "stop" or "break" in the nose; the Birman has a broad, rounded head, with a medium-length nose that does not have a stop; the British head is large and round, with full cheeks and only a slight nose stop; the Burmese has a rounded head, with wide cheeks, tapering to a short, blunt wedge and in profile shows a firm chin and distinct nose break; the Siamese has a long head, narrowing in straight lines to a fine muzzle and the profile should be straight

**Persian**

**Birman**

**British**

**Burmese**

**Siamese**

### – HOW TO USE THIS BOOK –

To help with the identification of different breeds, entries are ordered by length of fur and type of cat. In most cases these roughly equate with the registering system used by the Governing Council of the Cat Fancy (GCCF) in the UK, but with some exceptions. According to the GCCF, a semi-longhair that has an already existing shorthaired counterpart is registered and judged under the relevant shorthaired section in most cases; however in this book, as these breeds appear to be semi-longhaired they will be found with the Semi-longhaired group. Equally, in the GCCF's Longhaired (Persian) section, there is a shorthaired variety, which in this book has been put with the Shorthaired group. All breeds are cross-referenced with their GCCF categories. Plain, solid-coated breeds are referred to as "self colours", and these precede the patterned or "non-selfs".

#### KEY TO SYMBOLS

These symbols provide at-a-glance information on how much care a breed requires. The two categories – grooming and space – are divided into four grades. Within the grooming category for example, one quarter shaded indicates little grooming is required, total shading indicates the need for a great deal of grooming.

**Grooming    Space**

PERSIANS

# BLACK  BREED LONGHAIR-PERSIAN   COAT SELF COLOURS

The Black Persian is one of the oldest known of this group and still one of the most popular. As with all Persians, the type has changed radically since the first cats were brought over from Persia in Victorian times; their faces are shorter, their ears smaller and their coats much longer.

**TYPE** a medium-sized, cobby cat with small, wide-set ears, short face and large, lustrous,

deep-orange coloured eyes

**COAT** long and luxuriant, with a softer undercoat. In an adult, the coat should be a dense, solid black but kittens may show pale ghost tabby markings up to the age of about six months

**COLOURS** blue, chocolate, cream, lilac, red, white

**CHARACTER AND TEMPERAMENT** quiet, gentle, not generally demanding

**ASSOCIATED BREEDS** other Persians, Exotic Shorthair

**SHORTHAIR EQUIVALENT** Exotic Shorthair

**COUNTRY OF ORIGIN** Persia (now Iran)

**GCCF** Longhair (Persian)

10

# *B L U E*   BREED LONGHAIR-PERSIAN   COAT SELF COLOURS

Another of the earlier known colours, the Blue Persian is reputed to have been Queen Victoria's favourite breed of cat. It is still one of the most popular of the self colours and usually has a large number of entries at cat shows.

**TYPE** medium-sized, stocky but elegant, with a round head and short face; small, neat ears and large, lustrous golden or copper-coloured eyes

**COAT** long, thick, soft and fine; the colour should be a pale to medium blue, solid to the roots, without any shadings or markings

**COLOURS** black, chocolate, cream, lilac, red, white

**CHARACTER AND TEMPERAMENT** quiet, sweet-natured, loving and gentle

**ASSOCIATED BREEDS** other Persians, Exotic Shorthair

**SHORTHAIR EQUIVALENT** Exotic Shorthair

**COUNTRY OF ORIGIN** Persia (now Iran)

**GCCF** Longhair (Persian)

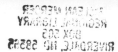

## CHOCOLATE BREED LONGHAIR-PERSIAN COAT SELF COLOURS

A relatively recent colour development, the Chocolate Persian emerged from the breeding programme devised to produce Colourpoint Persians; a glamorous breed in its own right, it is a useful outcross in Colourpoint breeding.

**TYPE** medium-sized, cobby but elegant; round, full-cheeked, short face; small, low-set ears and large, lustrous, deep-orange or copper-coloured eyes
**COAT** long, luxuriant, thick and silky; an even, warm, medium to dark chocolate in colour which should be free from shading or markings
**COLOURS** black, blue, cream, lilac, red, white
**CHARACTER AND TEMPERAMENT** gentle, affectionate and generally undemanding
**ASSOCIATED BREEDS** other Persians, Exotic Shorthair
**SHORTHAIR EQUIVALENT** Exotic Shorthair
**COUNTRY OF ORIGIN** UK
**GCCF** Longhair (Persian)

## CREAM BREED LONGHAIR-PERSIAN COAT SELF COLOURS

Known in the UK since the end of the 19th century, the Cream was not at first particularly popular, and was generally looked on as a rather poor, pale-coloured Red. Today, Creams are amongst the most popular of Persian colours both sides of the Atlantic.

**TYPE** medium-sized, cobby and elegant in body; a round, full-cheeked, short face; small, neat ears and large, lustrous, deep-orange or copper-coloured eyes
**COAT** long, luxuriant, soft and silky; the colour should be an even pale to medium cream, sound to the roots and free from shading or markings
**COLOURS** black, blue, chocolate, lilac, red, white
**CHARACTER AND TEMPERAMENT** friendly, affectionate, sweet-natured and generally undemanding
**ASSOCIATED BREEDS** other Persians, Exotic Shorthair
**SHORTHAIR EQUIVALENT** Exotic Shorthair
**COUNTRY OF ORIGIN** Persia (now Iran)
**GCCF** Longhair (Persian)

# *LILAC*  BREED **LONGHAIR-PERSIAN**  COAT **SELF COLOURS**

Like the Chocolate, the Lilac is a fairly new colour, created as a by-product of the Colourpoint breeding programme. Originally the breed was difficult to produce with the correct Persian type, but the problem has now been bred out and the delicate colour of the Lilac ensures it has a firm following of Fanciers.

**TYPE** as for all Persians, a medium-sized, cobby, elegant cat with the typical round, short face and full-cheeked expression; small neat ears and large, lustrous, deep-orange or copper-coloured eyes

**COAT** long, luxuriant, thick and silky; the colour should be an even, warm lilac, sound to the roots and without any shading or markings

**COLOURS** black, blue, chocolate, cream, red, white

**CHARACTER AND TEMPERAMENT** sweet-natured, friendly, affectionate and generally undemanding

**ASSOCIATED BREEDS** other Persians, Exotic Shorthair

**SHORTHAIR EQUIVALENT** Exotic Shorthair

**COUNTRY OF ORIGIN** UK

**GCCF** Longhair (Persian)

# *R E D*   BREED **LONGHAIR-PERSIAN**   COAT **SELF COLOURS**

One of the older established colours, a good Red is a very striking cat indeed. This is a difficult colour to breed as it is extremely hard to produce without unwanted tabby markings, and for this reason good examples are scarce.

**TYPE** medium-sized, cobby and elegant; the round, full-cheeked, short faced, with small, neat ears and large, lustrous copper-coloured eyes give the typical Persian expression

**COAT** long, luxuriant, thick and silky; the colour should be a sound, even, deep, rich red

**COLOURS** black, blue, chocolate, cream, lilac, white

**CHARACTER AND TEMPERAMENT** sweet-natured, gentle, friendly and generally undemanding

**ASSOCIATED BREEDS** other Persians, Exotic Shorthair

**SHORTHAIR EQUIVALENT** Exotic Shorthair

**COUNTRY OF ORIGIN** Persia (now Iran)

**GCCF** Longhair (Persian)

# *WHITE*   BREED LONGHAIR-PERSIAN   COAT SELF COLOURS

This breed comes in three varieties, each with its own breed number and the difference lies in the eye colour. White Persians may be Orange-eyed, Blue-eyed or the more unusual Odd-eyed. As the original longhaired white cats were the Angoras, popular before the longer-coated Persians were brought over to the UK, it is thought that the modern White Longhair is descended from cross-matings between these two varieties. Today, the Whites have the typical characteristics of this group, and bear no resemblance to the longer-faced Angora of yore.

**TYPE** medium-sized, cobby and elegant with a short, rounded face, full cheeks and large lustrous eyes; the eye colour should be a deep orange or copper in the Orange-eyed; deep blue in the Blue-eyed; and one eye of each of these colours in the Odd-eyed

**COAT** long, luxuriant, thick and silky; the colour should be a sparkling, pure white, with no shading or markings, although allowances are made for kittens, who may show some darker markings on the head which fade with maturity

**COLOURS** black, blue, chocolate, cream, lilac, red

**CHARACTER AND TEMPERAMENT** affectionate, friendly, and generally undemanding

**ASSOCIATED BREEDS** other Persians, Exotic Shorthair

**SHORTHAIR EQUIVALENT** Exotic Shorthair

**COUNTRY OF ORIGIN** UK

**GCCF** Longhair (Persian)

# *BI-COLOUR* BREED **LONGHAIR-PERSIAN** COAT **NON-SELF**

Although two-toned cats were known in the earliest days of the Cat Fancy, they were not particularly popular. With the development of the Tortie and Whites, Bi-colours would invariably crop up, and now they are accepted in all the recognized self colours both in the USA and the UK.

**TYPE** a medium-sized, well-muscled cat with a broad chest, wide, round head and short face; the ears are small, neat and wide-set; the eyes are large, round, deep orange or copper-coloured

**COAT** long, silky and luxuriant; the patches of colour should be well defined, the white parts

being between one-third to half of the body colour, and the face showing both colour and white

**COLOURS** black, blue, chocolate, cream, lilac, red

**CHARACTER AND TEMPERAMENT** sweet-natured, quiet, affectionate and generally undemanding

**ASSOCIATED BREEDS** other Persians, Exotic Shorthair

**SHORTHAIR EQUIVALENT** Exotic Shorthair

**COUNTRY OF ORIGIN** UK

**GCCF** Longhair (Persian)

# *BLUE CREAM* BREED **LONGHAIR-PERSIAN** COAT **NON-SELF**

Resulting from matings between Blue and Cream Persians, the Blue Cream is usually a female-only variety. In the UK the colours should be well mingled and in the

USA they should be patched.

**TYPE** medium-sized, well-muscled, with a broad chest; the head is wide and round and the face short; the ears are small and low-set; the eyes large and round, deep orange or copper in colour

**COAT** long, silky and luxuriant; the pastel blue and cream colours should be gently intermingled throughout the coat (UK) or patched (USA)

**COLOURS** no other

**CHARACTER AND TEMPERAMENT** sweet-natured, affectionate and generally undemanding

**ASSOCIATED BREEDS** other Persians, Exotic Shorthair

**SHORTHAIR EQUIVALENT** Exotic Shorthair

**COUNTRY OF ORIGIN** UK

**GCCF** Longhair (Persian)

# CAMEO BREED LONGHAIR-PERSIAN COAT NON-SELF

The Cameo is one of several tipped varieties of Persian and is midway between the heavily tipped Smoke and the more lightly tipped Chinchilla. The pale, near-white under-colour contrasts with the darker-coloured tips making a most attractively marked cat that is popular in all the Fancies.

**TYPE** medium-sized, well-muscled with a broad, deep chest; the head is wide and round, with a short face; the ears are small, neat and low-set; the eyes large, round, deep orange or copper-coloured

**COAT** long, silky and luxuriant; Cameos come in two forms, Shell and Shaded and in both the undercoat should be as white as possible, shading lightly toward the tips in the Shell, and more heavily in the Shaded

**COLOURS** red, cream or tortie

**CHARACTER AND TEMPERAMENT** sweet-natured, affectionate and generally undemanding

**ASSOCIATED BREEDS** other Persians, Exotic Shorthair

**SHORTHAIR EQUIVALENT** Exotic Shorthair

**COUNTRY OF ORIGIN** USA

**GCCF** Longhair (Persian)

# CHINCHILLA

With its sparkling silvery coat and large, emerald-coloured eyes, the Chinchilla has an almost ethereal look. Its distinctive, glamorous appearance makes it one of the most popular of the Persians.

**TYPE** medium-sized and cobby, with a broad, round head and small, well-tufted ears, and a brick-red snub nose outlined in black; the eyes are large, round and emerald green, and outlined in black giving the impression of mascara; this breed is usually more finely boned and elegant than other Persians
**COAT** long, dense and silky; the undercoat is pure white with evenly distributed black tipping, giving the typical sparkling silver appearance

**COLOURS** no other
**CHARACTER AND TEMPERAMENT** sweet-natured, affectionate and often more outgoing than most Persians
**ASSOCIATED BREEDS** Golden Persian, Shaded Silver, Exotic Shorthair
**SHORTHAIR EQUIVALENT** Exotic Shorthair
**COUNTRY OF ORIGIN** UK and USA
**GCCF** Longhair (Persian)

# COLOURPOINT (HIMALAYAN, USA) BREED LONGHAIR-PERSIAN COAT NON-SELF

By mating a Blue Persian to a Siamese, the Himalayan factor was introduced to the Persians, producing the restricted coat pattern usually only seen in Siamese. Available In a wide variety of colours and patterns, the Colourpoints are a popular addition to the Persian group.

**TYPE** medium-sized, cobby with a round, broad, short face; small, low-set ears and large, round, deep-blue eyes

**COAT** long, thick and silky; the points are restricted to the face, ears, paws, legs and tail

**COLOURS** seal, blue, chocolate, lilac, red, cream, and the associated colours of tortie, tabby and tortie-tabby (torbie USA)

**CHARACTER AND TEMPERAMENT** sweet-natured, affectionate and sometimes more outgoing and inquisitive than other Persians

**ASSOCIATED BREEDS** other Persians, Exotic Shorthair

**SHORTHAIR EQUIVALENT** Exotic Shorthair

**COUNTRY OF ORIGIN** UK

**GCCF** Longhair (Persian)

# GOLDEN PERSIAN BREED LONGHAIR-PERSIAN COAT NON-SELF

Now accepted as a breed in its own right, Golden Persians were originally called Golden Chinchillas as the colour was sometimes born to Chinchillas who carried the red gene. They are thought to have originated from Chinchillas that carried this gene and were imported into the UK from the USA. The Goldens are popular on both sides of the Atlantic.

**TYPE** a medium-sized, cobby cat with a broad, round head, snub nose, and small, well-tufted ears; the eyes are large and round, green or blue-green in colour

**COAT** long, dense and silky; the pale apricot undercoat shades to gold, the chest is pale apricot and the back, flanks, head and tail are a seal brown or black

**COLOURS** no other

**CHARACTER AND TEMPERAMENT** sweet-natured, affectionate, and loving

**ASSOCIATED BREEDS** other Persians, Exotic Shorthair

**SHORTHAIR EQUIVALENT** Exotic Shorthair

**COUNTRY OF ORIGIN** USA

**GCCF** Longhair (Persian)

# SHADED SILVER  BREED **LONGHAIR-PERSIAN**  COAT **NON-SELF**

The Shaded Silver is another tipped variety of Persian, but is more heavily tipped than the Chinchilla to which it is related. A useful outcross for breeding programmes, it is not a particularly popular breed in its own right.
**TYPE** medium-sized and cobby, with a broad, round head, small, wide-set and well tufted ears; large, round, emerald-green eyes
**COAT** long, thick and silky; a darker cat than the Chinchilla, the undercoat is pure white with the even, black tipping extending down one-third of the hair shaft

**COLOURS** no other
**CHARACTER AND TEMPERAMENT** sweet-natured, affectionate, friendly and often more outgoing than other Persians
**ASSOCIATED BREEDS** other Persians, Chinchilla, Exotic Shorthair
**SHORTHAIR EQUIVALENT** Exotic Shorthair
**COUNTRY OF ORIGIN** UK
**GCCF** Longhair (Persian)

# SMOKE  BREED **LONGHAIR-PERSIAN**  COAT **NON-SELF**

At first glance, the Smoke may appear to be a self colour but, when it moves, a glimmer of paler colour can be seen revealing the white under-colour. The most densely coloured of all the tipped varieties, the contrasting coat makes the Smoke a glamorous and popular breed.
**TYPE** medium-sized and cobby, with a broad, round head, snub nose and small, tufted ears; the eyes are large and round, deep orange or copper in colour
**COAT** long, dense and silky; the shading should be evenly distributed and almost to the roots, with the under-colour as near to white as possible
**COLOURS** black, blue, red, cream, chocolate, lilac and the four colours of tortie

**CHARACTER AND TEMPERAMENT** sweet-natured, affectionate and generally undemanding
**ASSOCIATED BREEDS** other Persians, Exotic Shorthair
**SHORTHAIR EQUIVALENT** Exotic Shorthair
**COUNTRY OF ORIGIN** UK
**GCCF** Longhair (Persian)

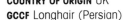

# *TABBY* BREED **LONGHAIR-PERSIAN** COAT **NON-SELF**

Tabbies were amongst the earliest known Persians. Today they are available in many different colours including the Tortie-tabbies, although the most commonly seen is the Brown Tabby.

**TYPE** a cobby, muscular cat with a broad, round head and short face; the ears are small, neat, low-set and well tufted; the eyes are large, and vary in colour from green to copper, depending on the coat colour

**COAT** long, dense and silky; the darker tabby markings should be distinct from the ground colour and should show an "M" marking on the forehead, a "butterfly" over the shoulders and "oysters" on the flanks

**COLOURS** brown, silver, red, blue, chocolate, lilac and the associated colours of tortie-tabby

**CHARACTER AND TEMPERAMENT** sweet-natured, affectionate and generally undemanding

**ASSOCIATED BREEDS** other Persians, Exotic Shorthair

**SHORTHAIR EQUIVALENT** Exotic Shorthair

**COUNTRY OF ORIGIN** Persia (now Iran)

**GCCF** Longhair (Persian)

# *TORTOISESHELL*   BREED LONGHAIR-PERSIAN   COAT NON-SELF

As with other tortie breeds, the longhair Tortie is usually a female-only variety – fertile males in this pattern are very rarely produced. A delightful breed in its own right, it is useful in producing Red and Cream Persians.
**TYPE** medium-sized, cobby and broad-chested; the head is round and broad with a short nose, the ears small and wide-set; the large round eyes deep orange or copper in colour
**COAT** long, thick and fine; the tortie markings should be well broken and evenly mixed throughout the coat

**COLOURS** black, blue, chocolate, lilac
**CHARACTER AND TEMPERAMENT** sweet-natured, affectionate and generally undemanding
**ASSOCIATED BREEDS** other Persians, Exotic Shorthair
**SHORTHAIR EQUIVALENT** Exotic Shorthair
**COUNTRY OF ORIGIN** UK
**GCCF** Longhair (Persian)

# *TORTIE & WHITE*   (CALICO, USA)  BREED LONGHAIR-PERSIAN   COAT NON-SELF

Originally known as the "Chintz" cat in the UK, and now called the Calico in the USA, the Tortie and White is an attractive and colourful variety of Persian frequently seen on the show bench.
**TYPE** medium-sized, cobby and broad-chested; the head is broad and round with a short nose; the ears small, neat and wide-set; the eyes large, round and deep orange or copper-coloured
**COAT** long, thick and fine; the coat should be between one-third and one-half white, broken with distinct patches of colour and the face showing both white and colour
**COLOURS** black, blue
**CHARACTER AND TEMPERAMENT** sweet-natured, friendly, affectionate and not generally demanding

**ASSOCIATED BREEDS** other Persians, Exotic Shorthair
**SHORTHAIR EQUIVALENT** Exotic Shorthair
**COUNTRY OF ORIGIN** UK
**GCCF** Longhair (Persian)

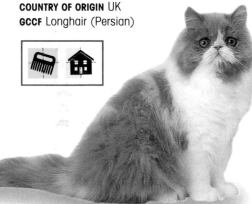

# PEKE-FACED BREED LONGHAIR-PERSIAN (USA ONLY)

An aptly named breed whose short, flattened face resembles that of a Pekinese dog, the Peke-faced is a uniquely American development. In the UK, some breeders produce very short-faced Persians called "Ultras", which, although similar to the Peke-faced, are not of such extreme type and are unrelated.

**TYPE** similar to that of the Persian, but with a snub nose, wrinkled muzzle and an indentation between the eyes

**COAT** as with all Persians, long, thick and luxuriant

**COLOURS** red tabby

**CHARACTER AND TEMPERAMENT** despite the rather cross expression, it is affectionate and sweet-natured

**ASSOCIATED BREEDS** none

**SHORTHAIR EQUIVALENT** none

**COUNTRY OF ORIGIN** USA

**GCCF** not available

# AMERICAN CURL   BREED SEMI-LONGHAIR

First seen in California in 1981, the American Curl has only recently been imported into the UK. The original Curl, Shulamith, was a stray with strangely curled-back ears, and when she produced a litter of kittens two of these had curled ears like their mother. A breeding plan was set up and now, 14 years later, this breed has championship status with the Cat Fanciers' Association (CFA) and a firm following in the USA.

**TYPE** medium-sized, elegant cat with distinctive curled-back ears curving in a smooth arc; the eyes are large and round

**COAT** medium-long and lying flat against the body; the tail should be full and the ears well furnished with fur

**COLOURS** all colours and patterns acceptable

**CHARACTER AND TEMPERAMENT** a friendly, intelligent, playful and companionable breed that does not insist on constant attention

**ASSOCIATED BREEDS** none

**SHORTHAIR EQUIVALENT** American Curl Shorthair

**COUNTRY OF ORIGIN** USA

**GCCF** as yet unrecognized but probably Foreign

# *ANGORA*   BREED SEMI-LONGHAIR

The original Angora cats were first seen in Victorian times and came from Ankara in Turkey. They lost popularity when the fuller-coated and more glamorous Persians arrived; those seen gracing the show benches today are a genetic recreation of the early Angoras, basically semi-longhaired Orientals.

**TYPE** like the Oriental, the Angora is a long, lithe and elegant cat, with a long, tapering wedge-shaped head, long straight nose and almond-shaped eyes

**COAT** long, silky, with a definite sheen, and a plume-like tail

**COLOURS** black, blue, chocolate, lilac, red, cream, cinnamon, caramel, fawn, tortie, tabby and white

**CHARACTER AND TEMPERAMENT** lively, intelligent and companionable

**ASSOCIATED BREEDS** Oriental, Siamese, Balinese

**SHORTHAIR EQUIVALENT** Oriental

**COUNTRY OF ORIGIN** UK

**GCCF** Oriental

# BALINESE   BREED SEMI-LONGHAIR

This semi-longhaired Siamese breed was first seen in a litter of Siamese kittens in the USA; when two of these kittens were mated together, they bred true and all the kittens had long, silky coats. The breed's popularity increased and by 1963 it was granted official recognition, but it was not until 30 years later that it achieved recognition in the UK.

**TYPE** as with the Siamese, the Balinese is a lithe, graceful breed with long, slim legs and a typical Siamese wedge-shaped head

**COAT** long, silky and fine textured; the tail should be plume-like and the ears may be tufted

**COLOURS** seal, blue, chocolate, lilac, red, cream, tortie and tabby (in the USA, the last four are known as **Javanese**)

**CHARACTER AND TEMPERAMENT** lively and intelligent, but slightly quieter and less boisterous than Siamese

**ASSOCIATED BREEDS** Siamese, Angora

**SHORTHAIR EQUIVALENT** Siamese

**COUNTRY OF ORIGIN** USA

**GCCF** Siamese

# BIRMAN BREED SEMI-LONGHAIR

A unique breed with distinctive white paws, the Birman originally came from Burma, where it was considered a sacred temple cat. It was imported to France in 1919 but did not reach the UK until the mid 1960s. It is now popular worldwide.

**TYPE** a long-bodied, elegant cat with a rounded head, full cheeks, medium-sized, well-spaced ears and blue eyes; the most distinctive feature of the Birman is its white paws

**COAT** long and silky, with a ruff around the neck and a bushy tail; the darker-coloured points, set against a pale body colour, should be restricted to the face, ears, tail and legs; the front and back paws are white

**COLOURS** seal, blue, chocolate, lilac, red, cream, tortie, tortie-tabby (torbie, in USA) and tabby

**CHARACTER AND TEMPERAMENT** intelligent, without being demanding or noisy

**ASSOCIATED BREEDS** none

**SHORTHAIR EQUIVALENT** none

**COUNTRY OF ORIGIN** Burma

**GCCF** Semi-longhair

# CYMRIC BREED SEMI-LONGHAIR

One of the few tailless, or short-tailed, breeds, the Cymric is the semi-longhaired version of the Manx. Popular in the USA, it is occasionally seen in Manx litters in the UK but has never established a following.

**TYPE** for show purposes, the Cymric should be completely tailless but, as with the Manx, stumpies and tailed versions can crop up; the breed type is that of modified British/American Shorthair, but the hind legs are longer than the front, which produces a curious rabbit-like gait

**COAT** thicker and longer than the Manx, but not as long as most other semi-longhairs

**COLOURS** accepted in any colour or pattern

**CHARACTER AND TEMPERAMENT** friendly and intelligent with a quiet voice

**ASSOCIATED BREEDS** Manx

**SHORTHAIR EQUIVALENT** Manx

**COUNTRY OF ORIGIN** Isle of Man (UK)

**GCCF** unrecognized at present, but probably British Shorthair (Manx)

# MAINE COON BREED SEMI-LONGHAIR

An all-American breed with a possible European connection; the Maine Coon is thought to be descended from the cats Marie-Antoinette sent to the New World to escape the French Revolution. It gained its name from the state of Maine, where it originated, while "Coon" reflects its racoon-like tail.

**TYPE** often referred to as the largest breed of cat, it is a sturdy breed with long legs, a long head and a squared-off muzzle

**COAT** waterproof, heavy, thick and dense, the coat is most prolific around the neck, giving a distinct ruff, and the belly, legs and tail; the ears and paws should be tufted

**COLOURS** accepted in almost any coat colour or pattern

**CHARACTER AND TEMPERAMENT** its size belies its sweet, friendly and playful nature

**ASSOCIATED BREEDS** none

**SHORTHAIR EQUIVALENT** none

**COUNTRY OF ORIGIN** USA

**GCCF** Semi-longhair

# NORWEGIAN FOREST CAT   BREED SEMI-LONGHAIR

Norse legends refer to a mountain-dwelling "fairy cat", able to climb almost sheer rock faces: this breed certainly has an ethereal look and is adept at climbing so perhaps the legend is true. A relative newcomer to the Cat Fancy, the Norwegian Forest Cat arrived in the UK in the late 1980s, and is now a popular breed in Europe and the USA.

**TYPE** a big, strong and solidly boned cat, with a long body, tall legs and a triangular-shaped face

**COAT** waterproof, thick, long and glossy covering a woolly undercoat, the coat is most prolific around the ruff, chest front and hind legs

**COLOURS** accepted in almost any coat colour or pattern

**CHARACTER AND TEMPERAMENT** lively, friendly and independent, this is a great hunter that enjoys access to a garden

**ASSOCIATED BREEDS** none

**SHORTHAIR EQUIVALENT** none

**COUNTRY OF ORIGIN** Norway

**GCCF** Semi-longhair

---

# RAGDOLL   BREED SEMI-LONGHAIR

Many flamboyant claims have been made about the background of this breed, but the ancestry of the Ragdoll is probably linked with Colourpoint Persians, Birmans and Siamese. As the name reflects, this sweet-natured breed loves to flop in your arms like a rag doll.

**TYPE** a long, muscular, broad-chested breed with heavy-boned legs, large, tufted paws and a large, flat-skulled head with rounded cheeks and large, oval, blue eyes; the ears are medium-sized and wide-set

**COAT** medium-length, silky, dense and close-lying fur, noticeably longer around the ruff and on the bushy tail; the restricted coat pattern comes in three forms, Colour-pointed, Mitted and Bi-colour

**COLOURS** seal, blue, chocolate and lilac

**CHARACTER AND TEMPERAMENT** generally easy-going, undemanding, quiet and gentle

**ASSOCIATED BREEDS** none

**SHORTHAIR EQUIVALENT** none

**COUNTRY OF ORIGIN** USA

**GCCF** Semi-longhair

# SOMALI  BREED SEMI-LONGHAIR

In the past, the occasional fluffy kittens found in litters of Abyssinians were generally considered to be poorly coated, shaggy examples of the breed and were "swept under the carpet". Today, the Somali is a popular breed with championship status in all countries.

**TYPE** a medium-sized, well-proportioned, firm and muscular cat; the head has a moderate wedge, the facial features round and well contoured; the eyes are almond-shaped

**COAT** a double coat of medium length, dense, fine and soft to the touch and with treble-banded ticking; more profuse fur around the ruff, tail and rear legs produces the Somali's typically "foxy" look

**COLOURS** usual, sorrel, chocolate, blue, lilac, fawn, silver

**CHARACTER AND TEMPERAMENT** intelligent, outgoing and companionable

**ASSOCIATED BREEDS** Abyssinian

**SHORTHAIR EQUIVALENT** Abyssinian

**COUNTRY OF ORIGIN** USA

**GCCF** Semi-longhair

# TIFFANIE BREED SEMI-LONGHAIR

In the UK the Tiffanie is the semi-longhaired version of a recently established breed known as the Asian group; in the USA the Tiffany is the semi-longhaired Burmese. Although physically similar, they are genetically quite distinct.

**TYPE** overall, the type should be similar to Burmese, with the eye colour varying from yellow through to green depending on coat colour

**COAT** silky and fine and long on the body particularly on the tail and neck ruff

**COLOURS** black, blue, chocolate, lilac, caramel, red, cream, apricot, and the associated torties; it is accepted in silver and standard versions and in full and Burmese expression; it may also be shaded, smoke, tabby or black self

**CHARACTER AND TEMPERAMENT** outgoing, friendly, sociable and athletic

**ASSOCIATED BREEDS** other Asians, Bombay, Burmilla

**SHORTHAIR EQUIVALENT** Asians, Bombay, Burmilla

**COUNTRY OF ORIGIN** UK

**GCCF** Foreign (Asian Group)

# *TURKISH VAN* BREED SEMI-LONGHAIR

Named after the Lake Van region in Turkey where it was first seen, this breed loves water, which is why it is often referred to as the Turkish Swimming Cat. First brought to the UK in the 1950s, it now enjoys championship status on both sides of the Atlantic.

**TYPE** a long, sturdy, muscular and strong breed with neat, tufted paws and a short, wedge-shaped head with a long, straight nose; the eye colouring orange, blue or odd-eyed

**COAT** long, soft and silky without a woolly undercoat; the body colour is chalk-white with markings restricted to the head, ears and tail

**COLOURS** auburn, cream

**CHARACTER AND TEMPERAMENT** friendly, intelligent, sociable and quiet-voiced; if you do not have a swimming pool, it will enjoy some exercise in the bath

**ASSOCIATED BREEDS** none

**SHORTHAIR EQUIVALENT** none

**COUNTRY OF ORIGIN** Turkey

**GCCF** Semi-longhair

## BRITISH BLACK   BREED SHORTHAIR-UK AND USA   COAT SELF COLOURS

Often considered the "native" British cat, the Black is just one of many colours and patterns within this group. It is thought that the first shorthairs came to England with the invading Romans, and that the British Shorthairs are their descendants.

**TYPE** a solid, cobby breed with a heavy feel; the head is large and round, ears small and neat and the eyes large and deep-copper coloured
**COAT** short, dense and with a glossy sheen; solid black to the roots with no sign of a rusty tinge
**COLOURS** blue, chocolate, cream, lilac, red, white
**CHARACTER AND TEMPERAMENT** "gentle giants", sweet-natured and generally undemanding – except when it comes to food!
**ASSOCIATED BREEDS** other British and American Shorthairs
**LONGHAIR EQUIVALENT** none
**COUNTRY OF ORIGIN** UK
**GCCF** British Shorthair

## BRITISH CHOCOLATE   BREED SHORTHAIR-UK AND USA   COAT SELF COLOURS

A relatively new colour of British which, like the lilac, is a by-product of the Colourpoint breeding programme; British Chocolates are often used as outcrosses for colourpoint as they commonly carry the gene for the restricted coat pattern.

**TYPE** cobby and solid, with a broad chest; the head is round and full-cheeked; the ears are small, neat and wide-set; the eyes are large, round, and yellow, orange or copper-coloured
**COAT** short and plush; the colour should be an even, rich, dark brown, solid to the roots with no shading or markings
**COLOURS** black, blue, cream, red, lilac, white
**CHARACTER AND TEMPERAMENT** sweet-natured, friendly, affectionate and generally undemanding
**ASSOCIATED BREEDS** other British and American Shorthairs
**LONGHAIR EQUIVALENT** none
**COUNTRY OF ORIGIN** UK
**GCCF** British Shorthair

# BRITISH BLUE    BREED SHORTHAIR-UK AND USA    COAT SELF COLOURS

The British Blue is one of the oldest of the self colours and today it is the best known of this group, and one of the most popular. With large, round eyes and a full-cheeked face, it has the sweetest expression, reflecting its gentle and kind disposition.

**TYPE** cobby and solid with a broad chest and a round, full-cheeked face; small, neat, wide-set ears and large, round, deep-orange or copper-coloured eyes

**COAT** short, dense and plush; the coat colour is an even light to medium blue, solid to the roots and without any shading, silvering or markings

**COLOURS** black, chocolate, lilac, red, cream, white

**CHARACTER AND TEMPERAMENT** sweet-natured, affectionate, generally undemanding but can have a voracious appetite

**ASSOCIATED BREEDS** other British and American Shorthairs
**LONGHAIR EQUIVALENT** none
**COUNTRY OF ORIGIN** UK
**GCCF** British Shorthair

# BRITISH CREAM BREED SHORTHAIR-UK AND USA COAT SELF COLOURS

The Cream is one of the more difficult colours to breed successfully. Early Creams were prone to undesirable tabby markings, but selective breeding has now minimized the fault, which is more obvious in summer, when the coat is shorter.

**TYPE** cobby and solid, with a broad chest; the head is short, round and full-cheeked; the ears are small, neat and low-set; the eyes large, round, deep yellow, orange or copper-coloured

**COAT** short, dense and plush; the colour should be an even, pale-toned cream and as free from markings as possible

**COLOURS** black, blue, chocolate, lilac, red, white

**CHARACTER AND TEMPERAMENT** sweet-natured, friendly, affectionate and generally undemanding, but with a hearty appetite

**ASSOCIATED BREEDS** other British and American Shorthairs

**LONGHAIR EQUIVALENT** none

**COUNTRY OF ORIGIN** UK

**GCCF** British Shorthair

# BRITISH LILAC
**BREED** SHORTHAIR-UK AND USA   COAT SELF COLOURS

Another newer colour resulting from the Colourpoint breeding programme, the Lilac has an attractive pinky grey coloured coat. It is becoming an increasingly popular colour and is often seen on the show benches in the UK.
**TYPE** cobby and solid, with a broad chest; the head is round and full-cheeked; the ears are small, neat and low-set; the eyes are large, round and deep orange or copper in colour
**COAT** short and plush; the coat colour is an even, solid, frosty grey with a pink tinge
**COLOURS** black, blue, chocolate, cream, red, white

**CHARACTER AND TEMPERAMENT** sweet-natured, friendly, affectionate and generally undemanding
**ASSOCIATED BREEDS** other British and American Shorthairs
**LONGHAIR EQUIVALENT** none
**COUNTRY OF ORIGIN** UK
**GCCF** British Shorthair

# BRITISH WHITE    BREED SHORTHAIR-UK AND USA    COAT SELF COLOURS

The British White, like the White Persian, comes in three different varieties, Orange-eyed, Blue-eyed and Odd-eyed, each with its own breed number. Adults of the breed have a pure, brilliant white coat, but kittens may show some pale markings on the head, and these can be a useful indication of the cat's genotype. A blue-based White kitten, for example, may show pale blue markings and a black-based, may show black markings – this is one of the few breeds that sometimes shows its genes stamped on its forehead.

**TYPE** cobby and solid, with a broad chest; the head is round and full-cheeked, with small, neat, wide-set ears; the large, round eyes may be deep orange or copper (for Orange-eyed), deep blue (for Blue-eyed), or one of each colour (for Odd-eyed)

**COAT** short, dense and plush; the colour should be a pure, brilliant white with no yellow tinges, although faint head markings are permissible in kittens

**COLOURS** black, blue, chocolate, lilac, red, cream

**CHARACTER AND TEMPERAMENT** sweet-natured, affectionate and generally undemanding, but with a hearty appetite

**ASSOCIATED BREEDS** other British and American Shorthairs

**LONGHAIR EQUIVALENT** none

**COUNTRY OF ORIGIN** UK

**GCCF** British Shorthair

# BRITISH BI-COLOUR   BREED SHORTHAIR-UK AND USA   COAT NON-SELF

Unlike their Persian relatives, the Bi-colour British Shorthairs have always been a popular variety. Their coats are a mixture of white and any of the recognized self colours.

**TYPE** cobby and solid; the head is broad and round, with full cheeks and small, neat, wide-set ears; the large, round eyes should be deep gold or copper-coloured

**COAT** short, dense and plush; a well defined mixture of white and any of the solid colours, the white should be preferably one-third, and no more than half of the body colour

**COLOURS** black, blue, chocolate, lilac, red, cream, tortie

**CHARACTER AND TEMPERAMENT** sweet-natured, affectionate and generally undemanding, but with a hefty appetite

**ASSOCIATED BREEDS** other British and American Shorthairs

**LONGHAIR EQUIVALENT** none

**COUNTRY OF ORIGIN** UK

**GCCF** British Shorthair

# BRITISH BLUE-CREAM BREED SHORTHAIR-UK AND USA COAT NON-SELF

A delicately coloured variety, the Blue-cream is a well-mingled mixture of blue and cream in the UK, whereas in the USA breed standards call for well-defined patches of colour.

**TYPE** cobby and solid with a broad, round head, full cheeks, and small, neat, wide-set ears; the eyes are large and round and should be deep orange or copper-coloured

**COAT** short, dense and plush; the blue and cream colours should be evenly mingled throughout the coat but a small, narrow blaze is permissible on the face and all four feet should show cream

**COLOURS** no other

**CHARACTER AND TEMPERAMENT** sweet-natured, friendly and affectionate, but with a hefty appetite

**ASSOCIATED BREEDS** other British and American Shorthairs

**LONGHAIR EQUIVALENT** none

**COUNTRY OF ORIGIN** UK

**GCCF** British Shorthair

## BRITISH COLOURPOINTED BREED SHORTHAIR-UK AND USA COAT NON-SELF

In the 1970s a structured breeding programme was devised to produce a cat of British type, but with the restricted Himalayan coat pattern of the Siamese. This factor was introduced by matings to Colourpoint Longhairs, as their type was much closer to that of the British than the longer-faced Siamese.

**TYPE** solid and cobby; the head is round and broad, with full cheeks, small, neat, wide-set ears; the eyes are large, round, deep blue
**COAT** short, dense and plush; there should be a good contrast between the body colour and the points, which should be restricted to the face, ears, tail, legs and paws
**COLOURS** seal, blue, chocolate, lilac, red, cream, and the associated colours of tortie, tabby and tortie-tabby (torbie, USA)
**CHARACTER AND TEMPERAMENT** sweet-natured, friendly, affectionate and sometimes more outgoing than other British

**ASSOCIATED BREEDS** other British and American Shorthairs
**LONGHAIR EQUIVALENT** none
**COUNTRY OF ORIGIN** UK
**GCCF** British Shorthair

## BRITISH SMOKE BREED SHORTHAIR-UK AND USA COAT NON-SELF

The first impression of a Smoke is often that it is a self coloured cat but, when the fur is gently moved, the pale, silvery undercoat is revealed. Available in a wide range of colours, the Black Smoke is probably the best known.

**TYPE** solid and cobby; the head is broad and round, with full cheeks; the ears are small, neat and wide-set; the eyes large, round, deep gold or copper-coloured
**COAT** short, dense and crisp; the darker colour overlies the silver undercoat, which is revealed when the fur is moved
**COLOURS** black, blue, chocolate, lilac, red, cream, tortie
**CHARACTER AND TEMPERAMENT** sweet-natured, affectionate and generally undemanding, except at meal times

**ASSOCIATED BREEDS** other British and American Shorthairs
**LONGHAIR EQUIVALENT** none
**COUNTRY OF ORIGIN** UK
**GCCF** British Shorthair

# BRITISH TABBY   BREED **SHORTHAIR-UK AND USA**   COAT **NON-SELF**

The tabby is one of the oldest known breeds of cat and within the British section it is bred in either classic or mackerel pattern and in a variety of colours.

**TYPE** solid and cobby, although the Silvers are sometimes more lightly boned; the head is broad and round, with full cheeks and small, neat, wide-set ears; the large, round eyes should be deep orange or copper-coloured in all colours except for the Silvers, where they should be green or hazel

**COAT** short, dense and plush; the classic pattern shows the typical "butterfly" over the shoulders and "oyster" markings on the flanks; the mackerel pattern shows a series of lines running vertically down the body; in both, the face should show an "M" mark on the forehead

**COLOURS** black, blue, brown, red and the associated silvers

**CHARACTER AND TEMPERAMENT** sweet-natured, friendly and affectionate

**ASSOCIATED BREEDS** other British and American Shorthairs

**LONGHAIR EQUIVALENT** none

**COUNTRY OF ORIGIN** UK

**GCCF** British Shorthair

## *BRITISH SPOTTED*   BREED SHORTHAIR-UK AND USA   COAT NON-SELF

Another, separately classified, tabby pattern and often considered the most glamorous. The spotted pattern is similar to that of the wild cats and has always been highly sought after.
**TYPE** solid and cobby, but sometimes more lightly boned, especially in the Silvers; the head is broad and round, with full cheeks and small, neat, wide-set ears; the eyes are large, round and deep orange in all but the Silvers, which should have green or hazel eyes
**COAT** short, dense and plush; the pattern should show well-distributed, numerous, distinct dark spots set off against a paler base colour; the tail is ringed and an "M" mark should be seen on the head
**COLOURS** black, blue, brown, red and the associated silvers

**CHARACTER AND TEMPERAMENT** sweet-natured, affectionate and generally undemanding, except when it comes to food
**ASSOCIATED BREEDS** other British and American Shorthairs
**LONGHAIR EQUIVALENT** none
**COUNTRY OF ORIGIN** UK
**GCCF** British Shorthair

## *BRITISH TIPPED*   BREED SHORTHAIR-UK AND USA   COAT NON-SELF

A relatively recent development, the Tipped was produced by introducing the Chinchilla into the British breeding programme. The result is a shorthaired cat of British type, but with the tipped coat so typical of the Chinchilla.
**TYPE** solid and cobby, but sometimes more lightly boned than other British; the head is broad and round, with small, neat, wide-set ears; the eyes are large, round and deep orange or copper-coloured except in Black Tipped, where they are green
**COAT** short, dense and plush; the undercoat is almost white with the evenly distributed tipping restricted to the end of the hairs, giving a sparkling effect
**COLOURS** black (silver), blue, chocolate, lilac,

red, cream, golden and the associated colours of tortie
**CHARACTER AND TEMPERAMENT** sweet-natured, affectionate and generally undemanding
**ASSOCIATED BREEDS** other British and American Shorthairs
**LONGHAIR EQUIVALENT** none
**COUNTRY OF ORIGIN** UK
**GCCF** British Shorthair

# BRITISH TORTOISESHELL BREED SHORTHAIR-UK AND USA COAT NON-SELF

A mixture of different colours makes for a most appealing cat, with the added distinction that no two Torties are ever alike. As with all tortie breeds, this is usually a female-only variety

and is bred In a wide range of colours.

**TYPE** solid and cobby; the head is short, round and broad with small, neat, wide-set ears and large, round, orange or copper-coloured eyes

**COAT** short, dense and plush; the colours should be even and well mingled but a facial blaze is permissible, and the feet should show cream; the American standards require well-defined patches of colour

**COLOURS** black, blue, chocolate, lilac

**CHARACTER AND TEMPERAMENT** sweet-natured, affectionate and generally undemanding, but tends to be greedy

**ASSOCIATED BREEDS** other British and American Shorthairs

**LONGHAIR EQUIVALENT** none

**COUNTRY OF ORIGIN** UK

**GCCF** British Shorthair

# AMERICAN SHORTHAIR BREED SHORTHAIR-UK AND USA

Similar to the British Shorthair, the American Shorthair has developed autonomously in North America but its ancestors probably came

over at the time of the Mayflower. In general, it is less "typey" than its British cousin, having a longer head and more rangy body.

**TYPE** a medium to large, muscular cat; the head is more elongated, legs longer, and ears larger than its British counterpart

**COAT** short, thick and hard; any softness in the coat is considered a severe fault

**COLOURS** accepted in almost any colour or pattern

**CHARACTER AND TEMPERAMENT** good-natured, intelligent, affectionate and outgoing, a good hunter

**ASSOCIATED BREEDS** British Shorthair

**LONGHAIR EQUIVALENT** none

**COUNTRY OF ORIGIN** USA

**GCCF** not available

# M A N X   BREED SHORTHAIR-UK AND USA

Although the Manx is classified in the UK under the British Shorthair section it is a quite distinct breed, with its own particular characteristics and traits. Originating from the Isle of Man, the history of this tailless breed is open to speculation, and the source of much legend. **TYPE** Manx come in three varieties, the completely tailless Rumpy, and the Stumpy and the Tailed which cannot be shown but are useful for breeding; this is a well-rounded cat, with back legs longer than the front, which give it a distinctive rabbit-like gait; the head is round, medium-long with a straight, wide nose and prominent cheeks

**COAT** double coated, with short, very thick fur; Manx need special attention paid to grooming
**COLOURS** all colours and patterns are acceptable
**CHARACTER AND TEMPERAMENT** intelligent, outgoing, affectionate
**ASSOCIATED BREEDS** Cymric
**SEMI-LONGHAIR EQUIVALENT** Cymric
**COUNTRY OF ORIGIN** Isle of Man (UK)
**GCCF** British Shorthair

# EXOTIC SHORTHAIR  BREED SHORTHAIR-UK AND USA

To the uninitiated, the Exotic Shorthair may look similar to a British, but this breed is really a shorthaired Longhair and should conform exactly to the standards laid down for Persian Longhairs except that it has a short coat. It is ideal for an owner who loves the Persian type, but cannot cope with grooming a long coat.

**TYPE** medium-sized and cobby; the head is round and massive, with a short, snub nose and small, low-set ears; the large, round eyes should be deep orange or copper-coloured except in the Silvers, where they should be green or hazel

**COAT** slightly longer than British Shorthairs, dense, plush and soft

**COLOURS** accepted in all colours recognized for Persians

**CHARACTER AND TEMPERAMENT** sweet-natured, affectionate and generally undemanding

**ASSOCIATED BREEDS** Longhair (Persian)

**LONGHAIR EQUIVALENT** Longhair (Persian)

**COUNTRY OF ORIGIN** USA

**GCCF** Longhair (Persian)

# *ABYSSINIAN* BREED SHORTHAIR-FOREIGN

The Abyssinian was first seen in the UK in the mid 1800s and is thought to have been brought over with traders visiting northeast Africa. Over the years the type of the cat has not changed radically, only the colour variations that are now available.

**TYPE** a medium-sized, elegant cat with long, slender legs, a round, wedge-shaped head and distinctive tufted tips to the ears

**COAT** short and close-lying with at least double ticking

**COLOURS** usual, sorrel, blue, silver, chocolate, lilac, fawn, red, cream, tortie

**CHARACTER AND TEMPERAMENT** sweet-natured, intelligent and outgoing, but will pine without company

**ASSOCIATED BREEDS** Somali

**SEMI-LONGHAIR EQUIVALENT** Somali

**COUNTRY OF ORIGIN** Abyssinia (now Ethiopia)

**GCCF** Foreign

# AMERICAN WIREHAIR BREED SHORTHAIR-FOREIGN

A natural mutation first seen in the mid 1960s in New York, the wavy-coated American Wirehair may, at first sight, seem to resemble the better-known Cornish Rex but they are completely unrelated. As yet unavailable in the UK, it is a popular breed in the USA, Canada and Europe.

**TYPE** a well-muscled, medium-sized cat with a round head, well-developed muzzle and large, round golden-coloured eyes

**COAT** short, coarse, thick and tightly crimped; to the touch, it is not dissimilar to a lamb's coat

**COLOURS** all colours and coat patterns are accepted

**CHARACTER AND TEMPERAMENT** friendly, inquisitive, affectionate and even-tempered

**ASSOCIATED BREEDS** none

**SEMI-LONGHAIR EQUIVALENT** none

**COUNTRY OF ORIGIN** USA

**GCCF** not available

# ASIAN SMOKE BREED SHORTHAIR-FOREIGN

Another member of the Asian group, the Smoke is a non-agouti cat with a pale, silvery or near-white undercoat and darker top coat. Originally called the "Burmoiré", the faint tabby markings give the impression of watered silk.

**TYPE** a shorthaired cat of Burmese type

**COAT** short and close-lying; the pale undercoat should reach one-third to half way up the hair shaft, the remaining part being darker; the forehead sometimes shows "frown" marks and the eyes may be ringed in silver which are sometimes referred to as "clown markings".

**COLOURS** black, blue, chocolate, lilac, caramel, red, cream, apricot and the associated torties; may be full or Burmese expression

**CHARACTER AND TEMPERAMENT** intelligent, friendly, playful, outgoing and acrobatic

**ASSOCIATED BREEDS** other Asians, Burmilla, Bombay and Tiffanie

**SEMI-LONGHAIR EQUIVALENT** Tiffanie

**COUNTRY OF ORIGIN** UK

**GCCF** Foreign (Asian Group)

# *ASIAN TABBY*  BREED **SHORTHAIR-FOREIGN**

This encompasses a wide range of patterned, shorthaired Asians. Accepted in four different patterns and in all colours, the ever-popular Tabbies are a great favourite within this group and there is choice enough for even the most discerning of cat owner.

**TYPE** a shorthaired out of Burmese type

**COAT** short and close-lying; it may be ticked, spotted, mackerel or classic in pattern

**COLOURS** black, blue, chocolate, lilac, caramel, red, cream, apricot and the associated tortie colours; these are accepted in silver or standard versions and in full or Burmese expression

**CHARACTER AND TEMPERAMENT** typical of this group, friendly, intelligent, playful and lively

**ASSOCIATED BREEDS** Asian Smoke, Burmilla, Bombay and Tiffanie

**SEMI-LONGHAIR EQUIVALENT** Tiffanie

**COUNTRY OF ORIGIN** UK

**GCCF** Foreign (Asian Group)

# BENGAL BREED SHORTHAIR-FOREIGN

In the early 1960s in the USA, an experimental mating took place between a domestic shorthair female and an Asian Leopard cat. It was not until the 1980s that a full breeding plan was implemented, the result of which is the Bengal, a spotted breed with a true wild-cat look, but the sweet disposition of a fireside moggie.

**TYPE** large and muscular, with the hindquarters slightly higher than the shoulders; the head is rounded, with prominent whisker pads and small wide-set, round-tipped ears giving the overall appearance of a small wild cat

**COAT** short, plush, unusually soft and pelt-like; spotted or marbled in pattern

**COLOURS** brown, cinnamon or snow

**CHARACTER AND TEMPERAMENT** friendly, loving, intelligent and inquisitive; this breed loves playing with water

**ASSOCIATED BREEDS** none

**SEMI-LONGHAIR EQUIVALENT** none

**COUNTRY OF ORIGIN** USA

**GCCF** pending, probably Foreign

# BOMBAY BREED SHORTHAIR-FOREIGN

The only shorthair self colour in the Asian group, the Bombay is a striking jet-black cat with golden-yellow eyes. In the USA, where they are referred to as "the patent-leather kids with the copper-penny eyes", the standard is slightly different as the Bombay is the self Black Burmese and is the result of mating Burmese with a Black American Shorthair.

**TYPE** a shorthaired cat of Burmese type

**COAT** short, close-lying and solid jet black to the roots, with a distinct sheen giving the appearance of shiny patent leather

**COLOURS** no other

**CHARACTER AND TEMPERAMENT** outgoing, affectionate, intelligent and acrobatic

**ASSOCIATED BREEDS** other Asians, Burmilla and Tiffanie

**SEMI-LONGHAIR EQUIVALENT** self Black Tiffanie

**COUNTRY OF ORIGIN** UK

**GCCF** Foreign (Asian Group)

# BURMILLA BREED SHORTHAIR-FOREIGN

Originating from an accidental mating between a Chinchilla male and a Lilac Burmese female owned by Baroness Miranda von Kirchberg, the first litter, which she named "Burmillas" were born in 1981. Today, their descendants are part of the popular new group which she developed known as the Asians.

**TYPE** a shorthaired cat of Burmese type but with differing coat colours and patterns

**COAT** the Burmilla has a short, shaded, close-lying coat

**COLOURS** black, blue, chocolate, lilac, caramel, red, cream, apricot and the associated torties; they are accepted in silver and standard versions, and in both full and Burmese expressions

**CHARACTER AND TEMPERAMENT** quieter and less demanding than Burmese, but more outgoing than Chinchillas; friendly, lively, intelligent, affectionate and somewhat athletic

**ASSOCIATED BREEDS** Asians, Bombay and Tiffanie

**SEMI-LONGHAIR EQUIVALENT** Tiffanie

**COUNTRY OF ORIGIN** UK

**GCCF** Foreign (Asian Group)

# CORNISH REX   BREED SHORTHAIR-FOREIGN

In the late 1950s a Cornish farmer discovered one curly-coated kitten in a litter born to a farm cat; his vet suggested that he mate him back to his mother to see what the result would be, and the kittens appeared with the same strange, curly coats. This was the natural mutation that gave rise to the popular breed known as the Cornish Rex.

**TYPE** a slender, muscular, medium-sized cat with a long, wedge-shaped head, flat skull, and large, high-set ears

**COAT** short, fine and soft in texture, the curly waves give a rippled appearance
**COLOURS** all coat colours and patterns acceptable
**CHARACTER AND TEMPERAMENT** lively, intelligent and active with a naughty side to their character
**ASSOCIATED BREEDS** none
**SEMI-LONGHAIR EQUIVALENT** none
**COUNTRY OF ORIGIN** UK
**GCCF** Foreign

# *DEVON REX*

A decade after the Cornish Rex was first seen in Cornwall in the late 1950s, a similar but genetically unrelated mutation occurred in Devon. Smaller, and with less dense curly fur, than the Cornish Rex, the Devon cats bred true when mated to each other and so were called the Devon Rex.

**TYPE** the body is firm, slender and muscular with long legs; the head is wedge-shaped, with full cheeks and large, low-set ears giving this breed the typical "pixie" expression

**COAT** short, fine and curled or waved; it is often not as thick as the Cornish Rex, but should never appear to be bald

**COLOURS** all coat colours and patterns are acceptable

**CHARACTER AND TEMPERAMENT** mischievous, intelligent, playful and friendly

**ASSOCIATED BREEDS** none

**SEMI-LONGHAIR EQUIVALENT** none

**COUNTRY OF ORIGIN** UK

**GCCF** Foreign

# EGYPTIAN MAU   BREED SHORTHAIR-FOREIGN

Despite its exotic sounding name, the Egyptian Mau has no connection with Egypt, but is an American breed designed to resemble the cats depicted in the Pharaohs' tombs. A spotted variety, similar to but less elongated than the Oriental Spotted Tabies in the UK, it is an elegant and glamorous feline.

**TYPE** modified Siamese, with a rounded wedge-shaped face, less angular than the Siamese

**COAT** short, smooth and close-lying with clearly defined spots

**COLOURS** black, smoke, pewter, bronze and silver

**CHARACTER AND TEMPERAMENT** intelligent, companionable, adventurous and outgoing

**ASSOCIATED BREEDS** none

**SEMI-LONGHAIR EQUIVALENT** none
**COUNTRY OF ORIGIN** USA
**GCCF** not available

# JAPANESE BOBTAIL   BREED SHORTHAIR-FOREIGN

Known in its native Japan as the "Mi-Ke", where it is considered a symbol of friendship, the Japanese Bobtail has a short "bobbed" tail which, typically, is carried upright when the cat is moving, but gently curls when it relaxes. As yet unavailable in the UK, it is popular both in the USA and in Japan.

**TYPE** its slender,dainty appearance belies a well-muscled, medium-sized body and, like the Manx, the hind legs are longer than the forelegs; the triangular-shaped head, and large, oval eyes give this breed a most appealing expression

**COAT** short and close-lying; the fur should radiate at the base of the tail

**COLOURS** typically tortie and white, but other colours acceptable

**CHARACTER AND TEMPERAMENT** friendly, intelligent, companionable

**ASSOCIATED BREEDS** none
**SEMI-LONGHAIR EQUIVALENT** none
**COUNTRY OF ORIGIN** Japan
**GCCF** not available

# *KORAT*   BREED **SHORTHAIR-FOREIGN**

The Korat is one of the oldest known breeds of cat and in its native Thailand is known as "Si-Sawat", the sacred cat and bringer of good fortune. Only seen in the original blue coat colour, the Korat came to the USA in the 1950s and to the UK in 1972, and it remains a popular breed on both sides of the Atlantic.

**TYPE** a medium-sized, muscular cat, the Korat has a heart-shaped face with lustrous, round eyes giving it a most sweet and appealing expression

**COAT** smooth and close-lying, but which should be broken along the spine

**COLOURS** a blue-only breed

**CHARACTER AND TEMPERAMENT** quiet, gentle, loving and intelligent

**ASSOCIATED BREEDS** none

**SEMI-LONGHAIR EQUIVALENT** none

**COUNTRY OF ORIGIN** Thailand

**GCCF** Foreign

# *OCICAT* BREED SHORTHAIR-FOREIGN

In the 1960s, an American breeder devised a breeding programme to produce Abysinnian Pointed Siamese by mating a Siamese to an Abyssinian female. She struck lucky in the second generation, but the much coveted Abyssinian point was not all she produced. Amongst an assortment of various tabbies was one golden-spotted male which looked just like a baby ocelot, and so the first Ocicat was born. Since 1987 this breed has had championship status in the USA, but it is still comparatively rare in the UK.

**TYPE** a long, solid, well-muscled cat with a broad head and muzzle and a suggestion of squareness to the jaw; the ears are large, wide-set and preferably tufted.

**COAT** short, smooth, sleek and well spotted

**COLOURS** brown, blue, chocolate, lilac, cinnamon, fawn, red, cream, torbie and silver of these colours

**CHARACTER AND TEMPERAMENT** intelligent, friendly, companionable

**ASSOCIATED BREEDS** none

**SEMI-LONGHAIR EQUIVALENT** none

**COUNTRY OF ORIGIN** USA

**GCCF** pending, probably Foreign

# *RUSSIAN BLUE* BREED SHORTHAIR-FOREIGN

Although white and black Russians have been seen occasionally, the Russian Blue is essentially a blue-only variety. Originally thought to have come from Arkangel'sk via the Baltic ports to England in the late 1800s, it was at first called the Archangel Cat. Because of their scarcity at this time, they were outcrossed to Siamese, but since their popularity has grown, such outcrosses have not been needed now for many years.

**TYPE** a medium- to large-sized, elegant, shorthair cat; its graceful movement on long, slim legs can be compared to a ballerina *en pointe;* the head is flat between large, high-set ears, with a straight profile and prominent whisker pads

**COAT** double-coated with short, thick, fine, soft and silky fur

**COLOURS** blue only

**CHARACTER AND TEMPERAMENT** quiet, gentle, intelligent, loving

**ASSOCIATED BREEDS** none

**SEMI-LONGHAIR EQUIVALENT** none

**COUNTRY OF ORIGIN** Russia

**GCCF** Foreign

# *SCOTTISH FOLD* BREED **SHORTHAIR-FOREIGN**

Originating from a natural mutation in Scotland in the 1960s, the Scottish Fold has distinctive ears which fold forward towards the face. Unaccepted in the UK, where the folded ears are considered detrimental to the cat's health, the Scottish Fold is a popular breed in the USA.
**TYPE** modified British, with a flatter skull and small ears that fold forwards; the eyes are large and round, giving an almost owl-like appearance
**COAT** thick and resilient, similar in texture to the Manx
**COLOURS** all colours acceptable
**CHARACTER AND TEMPERAMENT** despite the curious ears, this breed has perfectly normal hearing and is sweet-natured and gentle

**ASSOCIATED BREEDS** none
**SEMI-LONGHAIR EQUIVALENT** none
**COUNTRY OF ORIGIN** Scotland (UK)
**GCCF** not available

# *SINGAPURA* BREED **SHORTHAIR-FOREIGN**

Affectionately known as the "Singapore Drain Cat", the Singapura's lifestyle was originally that of a feral, scavenging in the back alleys and drains of Singapore; its ancestry is undocumented, but is likely to have been a mixture of the local, oriental-type cats mating with ships' cats visiting the port. In the late 1970s, the Singapura was imported to the USA, later to Europe and, most recently, to the UK.
**TYPE** improved, sensible husbandry makes today's Singapura a small- to medium-sized cat that should feel heavier than it looks; the head is rounded, with a blunt muzzle, the ears large and pointed, and the eyes large and almond-shaped
**COAT** short, ticked, tight, dense, smooth and silky
**COLOURS** brown ticked agouti sepia (USA)

**CHARACTER AND TEMPERAMENT** affectionate, friendly, playful and quiet in voice
**ASSOCIATED BREEDS** none
**SEMI-LONGHAIR EQUIVALENT** none
**COUNTRY OF ORIGIN** Singapore
**GCCF** as yet unrecognized, but probably Foreign

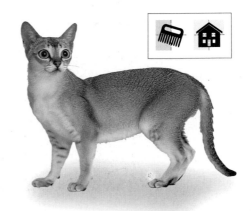

# *SNOWSHOE* BREED **SHORTHAIR-FOREIGN**

An American breed, the Snowshoe was developed in the 1960s by mating a Siamese with an American Shorthair Bi-colour. The result was a solidly built, shorthaired cat with a restricted Siamese coat pattern, but with distinctive white paws from the gene for low-grade white spotting introduced by the Bi-colour.

**TYPE** medium-large in body, with a triangular wedge-shaped face which should not be as long as the Siamese; eyes are blue and almond-shaped

**COAT** short, sleek and close-lying; mask, ears, tail and legs are darker while the paws and muzzle must be white, and a distinctive inverted "V" marking between the eyes is desirable

**COLOURS** seal, blue, tabby

**CHARACTER AND TEMPERAMENT** sweet-natured, intelligent, friendly

**ASSOCIATED BREEDS** none

**SEMI-LONGHAIR EQUIVALENT** none

**COUNTRY OF ORIGIN** USA

**GCCF** as yet unaccepted, but probably Foreign

# *SPHYNX* BREED SHORTHAIR-FOREIGN

Hairless breeds of cats have cropped up in various parts of the world from time to time, but it was not until 1966 in Canada that such a cat was born and the characteristics were thought worth perpetuating. The Sphynx is not completely hairless, but is covered in a very fine down giving it a velvety feel to the touch.
**TYPE** a medium-sized, muscular cat with long, slim legs, slender neck and a head that should be longer than it is wide
**COAT** although appearing hairless, the Sphynx is evenly covered in a soft, downy fur which may be denser on the legs and tail; the skin pigmentation and pattern should be clearly visible
**COLOURS** any colours and patterns acceptable
**CHARACTER AND TEMPERAMENT** outgoing, friendly, intelligent and mischievous

**ASSOCIATED BREEDS** none
**SEMI-LONGHAIR EQUIVALENT** none
**COUNTRY OF ORIGIN** Canada
**GCCF** as yet unaccepted, but probably Foreign

# *TONKINESE* BREED SHORTHAIR-FOREIGN

First developed in the USA in the late 1960s, the Tonkinese is a cross between a Siamese and a Burmese. The modern Tonkinese has the best characteristics of both of these founder breeds; it is an ideal choice if you love the Siamese personality but prefer the chunkier look of the old-fashioned Siamese type.
**TYPE** a well-muscled cat, the type of the Tonkinese should lie squarely between that of Siamese and Burmese without showing a tendency to either of the foundation breeds
**COAT** short, fine, close-lying, with a definite sheen
**COLOURS** brown, blue, chocolate, lilac, red, cream, and the associated torties, tabbies and tortie-tabbies (torbies, USA)
**CHARACTER AND TEMPERAMENT** intelligent,

friendly, outgoing and inquisitive
**ASSOCIATED BREEDS** none
**SEMI-LONGHAIR EQUIVALENT** none
**COUNTRY OF ORIGIN** USA
**GCCF** Foreign

# BLACK

Although it is recorded that a solid-black cat of Siamese type existed in Germany just before the Second World War, it was not until the early 1960s in England that thought was given to setting up a breeding programme to produce self-coloured Siamese. These are what we now call Orientals, and the Black is one of the most elegant and eye-catching of the self colours.

**TYPE** essentially, a Siamese-shaped cat masquerading under a solid, jet-black coat, but with green eyes

**COAT** short, glossy and close-lyng; the colour should be jet black to the roots with no rusty tinges

**COLOURS** blue, cream, havana, red, white, caramel, fawn, cinnamon, apricot

**CHARACTER AND TEMPERAMENT** intelligent, outgoing, affectionate and noisy

**ASSOCIATED BREEDS** other Orientals, Angora, Siamese, Balinese

**SEMI-LONGHAIR EQUIVALENT** Angora

**COUNTRY OF ORIGIN** UK

**GCCF** Oriental

# CINNAMON BREED ORIENTALS COAT SELF COLOURS

One of the newer colours, the Cinnamon was the result of introducing the sorrel gene from Siamese to Abysinnian matings in the late 1960s. The dilute version of this warm cinnamon-brown colour is known as Fawn.

**TYPE** medium-sized, long, slim, elegant and muscular, with the Siamese wedge-shaped head, long, slim legs and green eyes

**COAT** short, sleek and close-lying; the colour should be a warm cinnamon brown, solid to the roots, with no white hairs

**COLOURS** black, blue, cream, red, havana, white, caramel, fawn, apricot

**CHARACTER AND TEMPERAMENT** intelligent, outgoing, companionable, vociferous

**ASSOCIATED BREEDS** other Orientals, Angora, Siamese, Balinese

**SEMI-LONGHAIR EQUIVALENT** Angora
**COUNTRY OF ORIGIN** UK
**GCCF** Oriental

# CREAM BREED ORIENTALS COAT SELF COLOURS

Cream is one of the newer colours, and is the dilute version of Red. A useful addition to breeding programmes, when a Cream is mated to a Caramel it can produce Apricots.

**TYPE** medium-sized, slim, elegant and muscular, with the typical Siamese wedge-shaped head; the eye colour is preferably green, but may be any shade from copper through to green

**COAT** short, sleek and close-lying; the colour should be a cool, even cream, solid to the roots, with no white hairs

**COLOURS** black, blue, cinnamon, red, havana, white, caramel, fawn, apricot

**CHARACTER AND TEMPERAMENT** intelligent, outgoing, affectionate, vociferous

**ASSOCIATED BREEDS** other Orientals, Angora, Siamese, Balinese

**SEMI-LONGHAIR EQUIVALENT** Angora
**COUNTRY OF ORIGIN** UK
**GCCF** Oriental

# *HAVANA*  BREED **ORIENTALS**   COAT **SELF COLOURS**

In the early 1950s, breeders in the UK wanted to produce a chocolate-brown cat of Siamese type, and this was done by mating a Siamese to a half-Siamese black domestic female. In 1952, the first Havana was born and official breed recognition was granted in 1958.

**TYPE** medium sized, slim, muscular and elegant with a Siamese wedge-shaped head, long slim limbs and vivid green eyes

**COAT** short, sleek and close-lying; the colour is a solid, rich warm chestnut brown

**COLOURS** black, blue, cinnamon, cream, red, white, caramel, fawn, apricot

**CHARACTER AND TEMPERAMENT** intelligent, outgoing, companionable but with a loud voice

**ASSOCIATED BREEDS** other Orientals, Angora, Siamese, Balinese

**SEMI-LONGHAIR EQUIVALENT** Angora

**COUNTRY OF ORIGIN** UK

**GCCF** Oriental

# *WHITE*   BREED **ORIENTALS**   COAT **SELF COLOURS**

The only Oriental colour without green eyes, the White is a stunning, glacial white with piercing blue eyes. Unusually for this group, it is not often mated to other Orientals, but to Siamese, as this ensures the correct blue eye colour.
**TYPE** medium-sized, long, slim, elegant and muscular with long slim legs and brilliant blue eyes
**COAT** short, sleek and close-lying; the colour should be a pure, brilliant white
**COLOURS** black, blue, red, cream, havana, caramel, fawn, cinnamon, apricot

**CHARACTER AND TEMPERAMENT** intelligent, outgoing, companionable, vociferous
**ASSOCIATED BREEDS** other Orientals, Angora, Siamese, Balinese
**SEMI-LONGHAIR EQUIVALENT** Angora
**COUNTRY OF ORIGIN** UK
**GCCF** Oriental

# TABBY (CLASSIC) BREED **ORIENTALS** COAT **NON-SELF**

By mating Oriental to Tabby-point Siamese, it became possible to produce the Oriental Tabby, one pattern of which is the Classic. By further mating back to a Chinchilla Persian, the silver gene was introduced resulting in the glamorous Oriental Classic Silver Tabby.

**TYPE** a medium-sized, elegant but well-muscled cat of Siamese type in all but eye colour, which should be green

**COAT** sleek and close-lying, with a definite sheen. The markings should be clearly defined against the body colour

**COLOURS** brown, blue, chocolate, lilac, red, cream, cinnamon, caramel, fawn and the same in silver colours

**CHARACTER AND TEMPERAMENT** outgoing, intelligent and lively, this breed demands attention and is not afraid to use its voice to gain it

**ASSOCIATED BREEDS** Siamese

**SEMI-LONGHAIR EQUIVALENT** Angora

**COUNTRY OF ORIGIN** UK

**GCCF** Oriental

# TABBY (SPOTTED) BREED **ORIENTALS** COAT **NON-SELF**

The first recognized Tabby pattern in the Oriental section, the Spotted Tabby was first seen in the late 1960s. Until 1978, it was known in the UK as the Egyptian Mau, but its name was changed to avoid confusion with the American breed of the same name, which is unrelated and quite different.

**TYPE** as with the Siamese, this is an elegant, slim, well-muscled cat with a Siamese-shaped head, but with green eyes

**COAT** sleek and close-lying; the darker spots, which should be sound to the roots, round and evenly distributed on the paler-coloured coat; the breed may also be classic, mackerel or ticked

**COLOURS** brown, blue, chocolate, lilac, red, cream, cinnamon, caramel, fawn, apricot and the silver of these colours

**CHARACTER AND TEMPERAMENT** intelligent, outgoing, companionable and vociferous

**ASSOCIATED BREEDS** other Orientals, Angora, Siamese, Balinese

**SEMI-LONGHAIR EQUIVALENT** Angora

**COUNTRY OF ORIGIN** UK

**GCCF** Oriental

# *TABBY (TICKED)* BREED **ORIENTALS** COAT **NON-SELF**

Matings between Siamese and Abyssinians introduced the gene for ticking into the Oriental Tabby breeding programme and so gave rise to the Oriental Ticked Tabby. With its evenly ticked coat, reminiscent of its wild-cat ancestors, it soon became a popular pattern and was granted championship status in the UK in 1993.

**TYPE** medium-sized, long, slim and well-muscled with the typical Siamese wedge-shaped head, but with green eyes

**COAT** smooth, close-lying and evenly ticked with at least double, and preferably treble, ticking; it may also be in classic, mackerel or spotted patterns

**COLOURS** brown, blue, chocolate, lilac, red, cream, caramel, cinnamon, fawn, apricot and the silver of these colours

**CHARACTER AND TEMPERAMENT** intelligent, outgoing, companionable and loud-voiced

**ASSOCIATED BREEDS** other Orientals, Angora, Siamese, Balinese

**SEMI-LONGHAIR EQUIVALENT** Angora

**COUNTRY OF ORIGIN** UK

**GCCF** Oriental

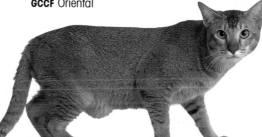

# *TORTOISESHELL* BREED **ORIENTALS** COAT **NON-SELF**

Part of the breeding programme that produced the self Red and Cream, the Tortie is usually a female-only variety although the rare, fertile male is occasionally seen.

**TYPE** a medium-sized, long, slim, elegant and muscular cat, with the Siamese wedge-shaped head and green eyes

**COAT** short and close-lying; the base colour should be solid to the roots, patched or mingled with red, cream, or rich beige

**COLOURS** black, blue, chocolate, lilac, cinnamon, caramel, fawn

**CHARACTER AND TEMPERAMENT** intelligent, outgoing, companionable, vociferous and with a "naughty tortie" sense of humour

**ASSOCIATED BREEDS** other Orientals, Angora, Siamese, Balinese

**SEMI-LONGHAIR EQUIVALENT** Angora

**COUNTRY OF ORIGIN** UK

**GCCF** Oriental

# TORTIE TABBY (TORBIE, USA) BREED ORIENTALS COAT NON-SELF

Oriental Tortie Tabbies are accepted in all four of the recognized Tabby patterns, and the Ticked Tortie Tabby, pictured, was the first of its kind to be registered in the UK. The distinctive coat is a mixture of tortie colours overlaid on a tabby background

**TYPE** medium-sized, long, slim, muscular and elegant, with a typical Siamese wedge-shaped head and green eyes

**COAT** short and close-lying; the tortie markings are masked by the tabby pattern, which is considered more important; the pattern may also be classic, mackerel or spotted

**COLOURS** black, blue, chocolate, lilac, caramel, cinnamon, fawn

**CHARACTER AND TEMPERAMENT** intelligent, outgoing, mischievous and vociferous

**ASSOCIATED BREEDS** other Orientals, Angora, Siamese, Balinese

**SEMI-LONGHAIR EQUIVALENT** Angora

**COUNTRY OF ORIGIN** UK

**GCCF** Oriental

# *BROWN BURMESE* (SABLE BURMESE, USA) BREED BURMESE

The first Burmese, Wong Mau, was brought from the Far East to California in 1930 and it was not until 1948 that the breed was imported into the UK. Today, Burmese are widely available throughout the world and are closely chasing Siamese in the popularity stakes.

**TYPE** a medium-sized, well-muscled breed, sturdy but elegant-looking; the head has a rounded dome and wide-set ears, and in profile, the nose should show a distinct break

**COAT** short and close-lying, with a glossy sheen; kittens are born a paler colour but in adulthood the coat should be a rich, warm, even brown with no "ghost" tabby markings

**COLOURS** blue, chocolate, lilac, red, cream, brown tortie, blue tortie, chocolate tortie, lilac tortie

**CHARACTER AND TEMPERAMENT** outgoing, intelligent, extrovert, this breed demands attention but is not as vociferous as Siamese

**ASSOCIATED BREEDS** Asian Group (UK), Tonkinese, Bombay (USA), Tiffany (USA), Malayan (USA)

**SEMI-LONGHAIR EQUIVALENT** Tiffany (USA)

**COUNTRY OF ORIGIN** Burma

**GCCF** Burmese

# *BLUE BURMESE* BREED BURMESE

The first Blue Burmese was born to Brown parents in the UK in 1955. Aptly named Sealcoat Blue Surprise, this silver grey kitten aroused much interest and proved, as had been suspected, that Burmese and Siamese shared a similar genetic background as Blue Point Siamese had been around many years.

**TYPE** well-muscled, medium-sized, sturdy and elegant, the head has a rounded dome, with wide-set ears and in profile should show a definite nose break

**COAT** short and close-lying with a distinct sheen; the colour should be a soft silver grey, with pronounced silvering on the face, ears and paws

**COLOURS** brown, chocolate, lilac, red, cream, brown tortie, blue tortie, chocolate tortie, lilac tortie

**CHARACTER AND TEMPERAMENT** friendly, affectionate, intelligent and playful

**ASSOCIATED BREEDS** Asian Group (UK), Tonkinese, Bombay (USA), Tiffany (USA), Malayan (USA)

**SEMI-LONGHAIR EQUIVALENT** Tiffany (USA)

**COUNTRY OF ORIGIN** UK

**GCCF** Burmese

# CHOCOLATE BURMESE (CHAMPAGNE, USA) BREED BURMESE

Two new dilute colours of Burmese, discovered in the USA, are the chocolate and lilac. In 1969–1972, cats carrying the chocolate gene were imported to the UK, where the Chocolate Burmese is now one of the most popular colours.

**TYPE** early Chocolates in the UK tended towards the chunkier American type; today, they conform to the general standard for all Burmese

**COAT** short and close-lying; the colour should be a warm, even, milk chocolate with allowances made for darker shading on the head, back and tail

**COLOURS** brown, blue, lilac, red, cream, brown tortie, blue tortie, chocolate tortie, lilac tortie

**CHARACTER AND TEMPERAMENT** intelligent, outgoing and friendly, the Chocolate Burmese is sometimes less demonstrative than the Browns and Blues

**ASSOCIATED BREEDS** Asian Group (UK), Tonkinese, Bombay, Tiffany (USA), Malayan (USA)

**SEMI-LONGHAIR EQUIVALENT** Tiffany (USA)

**COUNTRY OF ORIGIN** USA

**GCCF** Burmese

# *LILAC BURMESE* (PLATINUM, USA) BREED BURMESE

When a Chocolate Burmese also carries the recessive blue gene it becomes possible to produce a Lilac Burmese. Known as Platinum in America, this pale, pinky, dove-grey coloured cat is a popular addition to the spectrum of Burmese colours.

**TYPE** imported at the same time as the Chocolates, early Lilacs were chunkier than the British Burmese but today they are the elegant, muscular cat that we know as this breed

**COAT** short, sleek and close-lying; the colour should be an even, pale, dove grey with a distinct pinky tinge, which may be slightly darker on the face, back and tail

**COLOURS** brown, blue, chocolate, red, cream, brown tortie, blue tortie, chocolate tortie, lilac tortie

**CHARACTER AND TEMPERAMENT** friendly, intelligent and playful, it may be slightly quieter than the Brown or Blue

**ASSOCIATED BREEDS** Asian Group (UK), Tonkinese, Bombay, Tiffany (USA), Malayan (USA)

**SEMI-LONGHAIR EQUIVALENT** Tiffany (USA)

**COUNTRY OF ORIGIN** USA

**GCCF** Burmese

# RED BURMESE BREED BURMESE

Between 1965–1975, Burmese breeders in the UK created a whole range of exciting new colours. By introducing the red gene through matings with red tabby domestic shorthairs and Red Siamese, it made it possible for Burmese to be Red, Cream and Tortie-coated.

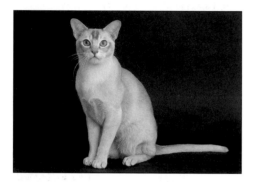

**TYPE** medium-sized, sturdy, well-muscled and elegant; the rounded dome, wide-set ears and distinct profile give the typical Burmese head
**COAT** short, sleek and close-lying; the colour should be a rich, light tangerine with slight tabby markings allowable on the face, and the ears darker than the back
**COLOURS** brown, blue, chocolate, lilac, cream, brown tortie, blue tortie, chocolate tortie, lilac tortie
**CHARACTER AND TEMPERAMENT** lively, outgoing, friendly and intelligent
**ASSOCIATED BREEDS** Asian Group (UK), Tonkinese, Bombay (USA), Tiffany (USA), Malayan (USA)
**SEMI-LONGHAIR EQUIVALENT**
Tiffany (USA)
**COUNTRY OF ORIGIN** UK
**GCCF** Burmese

# CREAM BURMESE BREED BURMESE

The Cream Burmese is a dilution of red and, along with this colour, can produce the spectrum of tortie colours. The rich, pale cream coat makes a most attractive addition to the plain-coated colours of Burmese.

**TYPE** medium-sized, well-muscled and elegant, with the typical Burmese head
**COAT** short, sleek and close-lying; a rich, even cream in colour, slight tabby marking is allowable on the face, slightly darker ears and a light "powdering" on the face, ears and paws
**COLOURS** brown, blue, chocolate, lilac, red, brown tortie, blue tortie, chocolate tortie, lilac tortie
**CHARACTER AND TEMPERAMENT** affectionate, lively, intelligent and outgoing
**ASSOCIATED BREEDS** Asian Group (UK), Tonkinese, Bombay (USA), Tiffany (USA), Malayan (USA)
**SEMI-LONGHAIR EQUIVALENT**
Tiffany (USA)
**COUNTRY OF ORIGIN** UK
**GCCF** Burmese

# *TORTOISESHELL BURMESE* BREED **BURMESE**

As with all Torties, this is usually a female-only variety and the majority of males are sterile. Possibly the most extrovert of all Burmese, they have not gained their nickname "naughty torties" without good reason.

**TYPE** medium-sized, strong and muscular, with the typical round domed head and distinctive profile of the Burmese

**COAT** short, sleek and close-lying; may be brown tortie, blue tortie, chocolate tortie or lilac tortie

**COLOURS** brown, blue, chocolate, lilac, red, cream

**CHARACTER AND TEMPERAMENT** intelligent, friendly, playful and outgoing but with a naughty sense of humour

**ASSOCIATED BREEDS** Asian Group (UK), Tonkinese, Bombay (USA), Tiffany (USA), Malayan (USA)

**SEMI-LONGHAIR EQUIVALENT** Tiffany (USA)

**COUNTRY OF ORIGIN** UK

**GCCF** Burmese

# SEAL-POINT BREED SIAMESE

With its distinctive darker-coloured "points" set off against a pale background, the Seal-point Siamese is probably the best known of all pedigree breeds of cat. Treasured in its native country, where it has been known for hundreds of years, it was often referred to as the "Royal Cat of Siam". It was first recorded at the Crystal Palace Show of 1874.

**TYPE** a medium-sized, long, slim, athletic and elegant breed with distinctive, piercing blue eyes; over the years, the Siamese has become more elongated and now has a long, wedge-shaped head and a long, thin whip-like tail

**COAT** short and close-lying with the dark seal-brown points restricted to the face, ears, tail, legs and paws

**COLOURS** blue, chocolate, lilac, red, cream, tabby (lynx, USA), tortie, tortie-tabby (torbie, USA), caramel, cinnamon, fawn, apricot

**CHARACTER AND TEMPERAMENT** outgoing, lively, intelligent and inquisitive, this breed has a loud voice that demands attention

**ASSOCIATED BREEDS** Orientals, Angora, Balinese, Colourpoint Shorthair (USA), Javanese (USA)

**SEMI-LONGHAIR EQUIVALENT** Balinese, Javanese (USA)
**COUNTRY OF ORIGIN** Siam (now Thailand)
**GCCF** Siamese

# *BLUE-POINT* BREED SIAMESE

The Blue-point made its debut at a show in 1896. Thought of as a poorly coloured Seal-point, it was not until the 1930s that breeders seriously campaigned this colour, which received its recognition in the UK in 1939. **TYPE** medium-sized, long, slim, muscular and elegant, with a long, flat-profiled, wedge-shaped head; large, wide-set ears and blue eyes

**COAT** short and close-lying, with the light blue points restricted to face, ears, tail, legs and paws
**COLOURS** seal, chocolate, lilac, red, cream, tortie, tabby (lynx, USA), tortie-tabby (torbie, USA), caramel, cinnamon, fawn, apricot
**CHARACTER AND TEMPERAMENT** intelligent, outgoing, playful, lively and vociferous
**ASSOCIATED BREEDS** Orientals, Angora, Balinese, Colourpoint Shorthair (USA), Javanese (USA)
**SEMI-LONGHAIR EQUIVALENT** Balinese, Javanese (USA)
**COUNTRY OF ORIGIN** UK
**GCCF** Siamese

## *CHOCOLATE-POINT* BREED SIAMESE

The first Chocolate-point was recorded in 1931 and, like the Blue-point, was considered a poor Seal. After two decades of breeding, it was finally afforded the status of its own breed number in 1950 in the UK and the official name of Chocolate-point.

**TYPE** medium-sized, long, slim, elegant and muscular, with a wedge-shaped face and long, straight profile; large, wide-set ears and blue eyes

**COAT** short and close-lyng, with the milk-chocolate coloured points restricted to the head, ears, tail, legs and paws

**COLOURS** seal, blue, lilac, red, cream, tortie, tabby (lynx, USA), tortie-tabby (torbie, USA), caramel, fawn, cinnamon, apricot

**CHARACTER AND TEMPERAMENT** intelligent, playful, companionable and vociferous

**ASSOCIATED BREEDS** Orientals, Angora, Balinese, Colourpoint Shorthair (USA), Javanese (USA)
**SEMI-LONGHAIR EQUIVALENT** Balinese, Javanese (USA)
**COUNTRY OF ORIGIN** UK
**GCCF** Siamese

## *LILAC-POINT* BREED SIAMESE

Once Blue- and Chocolate-points were in existence, it is quite likely that Lilac-points did occur naturally, but it was the introduction of Russian Blue to the Siamese line in the late 1940s that set this colour on a firm footing

**TYPE** medium-sized, long, slim, elegant and muscular, with a long, wedge-shaped face, flat in profile; large, wide-set ears and blue eyes

**COAT** short and close-lying with the pale, pinkish-grey points restricted to the face, ears, tail, legs and paws

**COLOURS** seal, blue, chocolate, red, cream, tortie, tabby (lynx, USA), tortie-tabby (torbie, USA), caramel, cinnamon, fawn, apricot

**CHARACTER AND TEMPERAMENT** intelligent, outgoing, companionable and vociferous

**ASSOCIATED BREEDS** Orientals, Angora, Balinese, Colourpoint Shorthair (USA), Javanese (USA)
**SEMI-LONGHAIR EQUIVALENT** Balinese, Javanese (USA)
**COUNTRY OF ORIGIN** UK
**GCCF** Siamese

# *RED-POINT* BREED SIAMESE

First exhibited in 1934, the Red-point was the product of introducing a domestic tortoiseshell into the Siamese breeding programme. More than 30 years later in 1966, it was granted recognition in the UK.

**TYPE** medium-sized, long, slim, elegant and muscular with a long, wedge-shaped face and straight profile; large, low-set ears and blue eyes

**COAT** short and close-lying, with the bright, reddish gold points restricted to the face, ears, tail, legs and paws

**COLOURS** seal, blue, chocolate, lilac, cream, tortie, tabby (lynx, USA), tortie tabby (torbie, USA), caramel, cinnamon, fawn, apricot

**CHARACTER AND TEMPERAMENT** intelligent, outgoing, companionable, playful and vociferous

**ASSOCIATED BREEDS** Orientals, Angora, Balinese, Colourpoint Shorthair (USA), Javanese (USA)

**SEMI-LONGHAIR EQUIVALENT** Balinese, Javanese (USA)

**COUNTRY OF ORIGIN** UK

**GCCF** Siamese

# CREAM-POINT BREED SIAMESE

It was inevitable that once the Red-point Siamese was established, its natural dilution the paler-coloured Cream-point would follow. Lightest of all Siamese colours, it gained recognition in the UK in 1966.

**TYPE** medium-sized, long, slim, elegant and muscular with a long, wedge-shaped head and straight profile; large, wide-set ears and blue eyes

**COAT** short and close-lying, with the cream points on the face, ears, tail, legs and paws

**COLOURS** seal, blue, chocolate, lilac, red, tortie, tabby (lynx, USA), tortie tabby (torbie, USA), caramel, cinnamon, fawn, apricot

**CHARACTER AND TEMPERAMENT** intelligent, playful, companionable and vociferous

**ASSOCIATED BREEDS** Orientals, Angora, Balinese Colourpoint Shorthair (USA), Javanese (USA)

**SEMI-LONGHAIR EQUIVALENT** Balinese, Javanese (USA)
**COUNTRY OF ORIGIN** UK
**GCCF** Siamese

# TORTIE-POINT BREED SIAMESE

Tortoiseshell cats are usually a female-only variety, with the occasional resulting male often proving to be sterile, and Tortie-point Siamese are no exception. Popular in its own right, the Tortie-point is also instrumental in producing the Red- and Cream-point Siamese.

**TYPE** medium-sized, long, slim, muscular and elegant, with a long, wedge-shaped head and

straight profile; large, wide-set ears and blue eyes

**COAT** short and close-lying; the colour, restricted to the face, ears, tail, legs and paws, is an evenly broken mixture of any of the recognized solid colours mingled with red or cream

**COLOURS** seal, blue, chocolate, lilac, red, cream, tabby (lynx, USA), tortie-tabby (Torbie, USA), caramel, cinnamon, fawn, apricot

**CHARACTER AND TEMPERAMENT** intelligent, extrovert, companionable and vociferous

**ASSOCIATED BREEDS** Orientals, Angora, Balinese, Colourpoint Shorthair (USA), Javanese (USA)

**SEMI-LONGHAIR EQUIVALENT** Balinese, Javanese (USA)
**COUNTRY OF ORIGIN** UK
**GCCF** Siamese

# *TABBY-POINT* (LYNX-POINT, USA) BREED SIAMESE

First recorded as early as 1902, it was not until 1961 that a litter of Tabby-points was shown and created quite a stir. Originally known as Shadow-points, and later Lynx-points, they were granted recognition as Tabby-points in 1966 in the UK, but are still known as Lynx-points in the USA

**TYPE** medium-sized, long, slim, muscular and elegant, with a long, wedge-shaped face and straight profile; wide-set ears and blue eyes

**COAT** short and close-lying; the points, accepted in the tabby pattern of any of the recognized solid and tortie colours, are restricted to the face, ears, tail, legs and paws

**COLOURS** seal, blue, chocolate, lilac, red, cream, tortie, tortie-tabby (torbie, USA), caramel, cinnamon, fawn, apricot

**CHARACTER AND TEMPERAMENT** intelligent, outgoing, companionable, mischievous and vociferous

**ASSOCIATED BREEDS** Orientals, Angora, Balinese, Colourpoint Shorthair (USA), Javanese (USA)

**SEMI-LONGHAIR EQUIVALENT** Balinese, Javanese (USA)

**COUNTRY OF ORIGIN** UK

**GCCF** Siamese

# INDEX

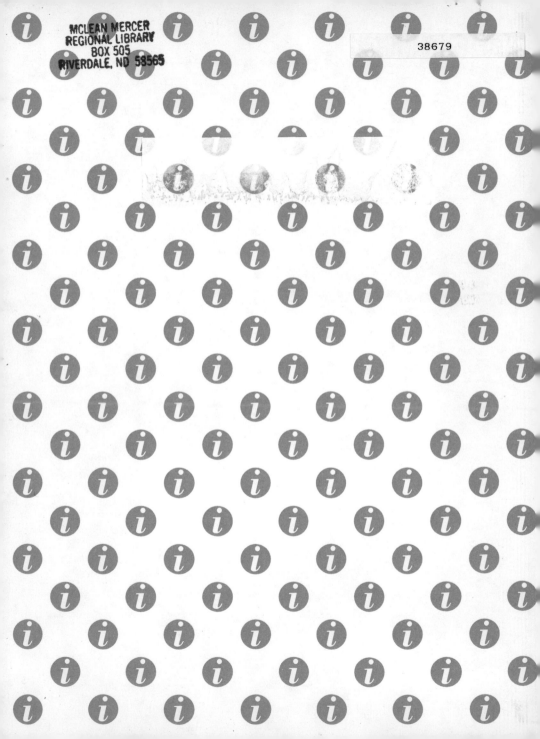